That All People May Be One People,
Send Rain to Wash the Face of the Earth

That All People
May Be One People,
Send Rain to Wash
the Face of the Earth

**Chief Joseph
1879**

That All People May Be One People,
Send Rain to Wash the Face of the Earth
Chief Joseph
1879

Published by Mountain Meadow Press
          P.O. Box 447
          Kooskia ID 83539-0447
          208-926-7875
© 1995 by Mountain Meadow Press

First Edition
Second Printing
Printed in the United States of America
ISBN 0-945519-15-X

Joseph, Nez Perce Chief, 1840-1904.
    That all people may be one people, send rain to wash the face of the earth / Chief Joseph.
    p. cm.
    Preassigned LCCN: 94-077351
    ISBN 0-945519-15-X

    1. Nez Perce Indians--Government relations. 2. Joseph, Nez Perce Chief, 1840-1904--Interviews. 3. Nez Perce Indians--Wars, 1877.   I. Title.

E99.N5   970.004'974
                                  QB194-20760

Contents

Credits

Text distilled from interviews originally printed in
the *North American Review*, April 1879.

Cover—Smithsonian Institution photo #2978-B.

Chief Joseph photo—Library of Congress

Clip Art © 1988-1992, Dream Maker

Clip Art © 1990-1992, RT Computer Graphics

Introduction

In 1805, Nez Perce Indians welcomed to their homeland a small party of sick and starving men led by Captains Meriwether Lewis and William Clark. "We are poor, but our hearts are good," Nez Perce chiefs advised Clark, as recorded in his journal. While the Nez Perces were "the most friendly, honest, and ingenious people that we have seen in the course of our voyage and travels," according to expedition member Sergeant Gass' records, and while their existence may have been humble, they were not poor. Their territory spanned from the Bitterroot Mountains of western Montana to the Wallowas of eastern Oregon. Their region was rich with fish, game, roots, berries, and the spiritual and cultural heritage of their ancestors. Within the next seventy-two years, however, the Nez Perces' homeland would be reduced by ninety-five percent and its people divided and indeed, in a much truer sense, poor. The culminating event of this process was the four-month long, 1300-mile Nez Perce War of 1877. While the war was waged largely under the leadership of Chief Looking Glass, it was In-mut-too-yah-lat-lat (Thunder Traveling Over the Mountains), known to whites as Chief Joseph, whose surrender forty miles from the sanctuary of Canada closed the war. "Our chiefs are killed," he reportedly said, "...

It is cold and we have no blankets. The little children are freezing to death. Some of my people have run away to the hills and have no blankets, no food; no one knows where they are — perhaps freezing to death. I want to have time to look for my children and see how many I can find. Maybe I shall find them among the dead.

Hear me, my chiefs. I am tired; my heart is sick and sad.

In 1879, Chief Joseph journeyed to Washington D.C. to attempt to negotiate a return to his homeland for those Nez Perces who had survived the war and were being kept on a reservation in Oklahoma. While in Washington, he granted reporters an interview, the contents of which comprises the text of this book. This, then, is Chief Joseph's own story, as given through an interpreter and first reported in the *North American Review*, April 1879. Readers today, as then, find herein truths of America's past and messages for America's future.

In-mut-too-yah-lat-lat
Chief Joseph

That All People
May Be One People,
Send Rain to Wash
the Face of the Earth

My friends, I have been asked to show you my heart. I am glad to have a chance to do so. I want the white people to understand my people. What I have to say will come from my heart, and I will speak with a straight tongue. Ah-cum-kin-i-ma-me-hut (the Great Spirit) is looking at me and will hear me.

My name is In-mut-too-yah-lat-lat (Thunder-Traveling-Over-the-Mountains). I am chief of the Wal-lam-wat-kin band of Chute-pa-lu, or Nez Perces (nose-pierced Indians). I was born thirty-eight winters ago. My father was chief before me. When a young man he was called "Joseph" by Mr. Spalding, a missionary. My father died a few years ago. There was no stain on his hands of the blood of a white man. He left a good name on the earth. He advised me well for my people.

Our fathers gave us many laws, which they had learned from their fathers. These laws were good. They told us to treat all men as they treated us, that we should never be the first to break a bargain, that we should only speak the truth, that it was a shame for one man to take from another his wife or his property without paying for it. We were taught to believe that the Great Spirit sees and hears everything, that He never forgets, and that hereafter He will give every man a spirit-home. If he has been a good man, he will have a good home; if a bad man, he will have a bad home. This I believe, and all my people believe the same.

We did not know there were other people besides the Indian until about one hundred winters ago, when some men with white faces came to our country. They brought many things with them to trade for furs and skins. They brought tobacco, which was new to us. They brought guns with flintstones on them, which frightened our women and children. Our people could not talk with these white-faced men but used signs which all people understood. These men were Frenchmen, and they called our people "Nez Perces" because we wore rings in our noses for ornaments. Although very few of our people wear them now, we are still called by the same name. These French trappers said a great many things to our fathers, which have been planted in our hearts. They told us some truths and some lies. Some were good for us; some were bad. Our people were divided in opinion about these men.

The first white men of your people who came to our country were named Lewis and Clark [1805-1806]. They also brought many things that our people had never seen. They talked straight, and our people gave them a great feast as proof that our hearts were friendly. These men were very kind. They made presents to our chiefs, and our people made presents to them. We had a great many horses of which we gave them what they needed, and they gave us guns and tobacco in return. All the Nez Perces made friends with Lewis and Clark and agreed to let them pass through our country and never to make war on white men. This promise the Nez Perces have never broken. No white man can accuse us of bad faith and speak with a straight tongue. It has always been the pride of the Nez Perces that they were the friends of the white men.

When my father was a young man, there came to our country a white man [Rev. Mr. Spalding, 1836] who talked spirit law. He won the affections of our people because he spoke good things to them. At first he did not say anything about white men wanting to settle on our lands. Nothing was said about that until about twenty winters ago when a number of white people came into our country and built houses and made farms. At first our people made no complaint. They thought there was room enough for all to live in peace, and they were learning many things from the white men that seemed to be good. But we soon found that the white men were growing rich very fast and were greedy to possess everything the Indian had. My father was the first to see through the schemes of the white men, and he warned his tribe to be careful about trading with them. He had a suspicion of men who seemed so anxious to make money. I was a boy then, but I remember well my father's caution. He had sharper eyes than the rest of our people.

Next there came a white officer [Governor Stevens] who invited all the Nez Perces to a treaty council [1855]. After the council was opened, he made known his heart. He said there were a great many white people in the country, and many more would come, and that he wanted the land marked out so that the Indians and white men could be separated. If they were to live in peace, it was necessary, he said, that the Indians should have a country set apart for them, and in that country they must stay. My father, who represented his band, refused to have anything to do with the council because he wished to be a free man. He claimed that no man owned any part of the earth, and a man could not sell what was not his own.

Eight years later was the next treaty council. A chief called Lawyer, because he was a great talker, took the lead in this council and sold nearly all of the Nez Perces' country. In this treaty Lawyer acted without authority from our band. He had no right to sell the Wallowa country. That had always belonged to my father's own people, and the other bands had never disputed our right to it. No other Indians ever claimed Wallowa.

In order to have all people understand how much land we owned, my father planted poles around it and said, "Inside is the home of my people—the white man may take the land outside. Inside this boundary all our people were born. It circles the graves of our fathers, and we will never give up these graves to any man."

We continued to live on our land in peace until eight years ago when white men began to come inside the bounds my father had set. We warned them against this great wrong, but they would not leave our land. The white men said that we were going on the warpath. They reported many things that were false. The United States Government asked for another treaty council.

My father had become blind and feeble. He could no longer speak for his people. It was then I took my father's place as chief. In this council I made my first speech to white men. I said to the agent who held the council, "I did not want to come to this council, but I came hoping that we could save blood. The white man has no right to take our country. We have never accepted presents from the government. Neither Lawyer nor any other chief had authority to sell this land. It has always belonged to my people. It came to them from our fathers. We will defend this land as long as a drop of Indian blood warms the hearts of our men."

The agent said he had orders from the Great White Chief at Washington for us to move to the Lapwai Reservation, and that if we obeyed, he would help us in many ways. "You must move to the agency," he said. I answered him, "I will not. I do not need your help. We have plenty, and we are contented and happy if the white man will leave us alone. The reservation is too small for so many people with all their stock. You can keep your presents. We can go to your towns and pay for all we need. We have plenty of horses and cattle to sell, and we won't have any help from you. We are free now; we can go where we please. Our fathers were born here. Here they lived, here they died, here are their graves. We will never leave them." The agent went away, and we had peace for awhile.

Soon after this my father sent for me. I saw he was dying. I took his hand in mine. He said, "My son, my body is returning to my mother earth, and my spirit is going very soon to see the Great Spirit Chief. When I am gone, think of your country. You are the chief of these people. They look to you to guide them. Always remember that your father never sold his country. You must stop your ears whenever you are asked to sign a treaty selling your home. A few years more and white men will be all around you. They have their eyes on this land. My son, never forget my dying words. This country holds your father's body. Never sell the bones of your father and your mother." I pressed my father's hand and told him that I would protect his grave with my life. My father smiled and passed away to the spirit-land.

I buried him in that beautiful valley of winding waters. I love that land more than all the rest of the world. A man who would not love his father's grave is worse than a wild animal.

For a short time we lived quietly. But this could not last. White men had found gold in the mountains around the land of the winding water. They stole many horses from us, which we could not get back because we were Indians. The white men told lies for each other. They drove off a great many of our cattle. Some white men branded our young cattle so they could claim them. We had no friend who would plead our cause before the law councils. It seemed to me that some of the white men in Wallowa were doing these things on purpose to get up a war. They knew that we were not strong enough to fight them. I labored hard to avoid trouble and bloodshed. We gave up some of our country to the white men, thinking that then we could have peace. We were mistaken. The white men would not let us alone. We could have avenged our wrongs many times, but we did not. When the white men were few and we were strong, we could have killed them off, but the Nez Perces wish to live at peace.

If we have not done so, we have not been to blame. I believe that the old treaty has never been correctly reported. If we ever owned the land, we own it still, for we never sold it. In the treaty councils the commissioners have claimed that our country had been sold to the government. Suppose a white man should come to me and say, "Joseph, I like your horses, and I want to buy them." I say to him, "No, my horses suit me; I will not sell them." Then he goes to my neighbor and says to him, "Joseph has some good horses. I want to buy them, but he refuses to sell." My neighbor answers, "Pay me the money, and I will sell you Joseph's horses." The white man returns to me and says, "Joseph, I have bought your horses, and you must let me have them." If we sold our lands to the government, this is the way they were bought.

Through all the years since the white man came to Wallowa, we have been threatened and taunted by them and the treaty Nez Perces. They have given us no rest. We have had a few good friends among white men, and they have always advised my people to bear these taunts without fighting. Our young men were quick-tempered, and I have had great trouble in keeping them from doing rash things. I have carried a heavy load on my back ever since I was a boy. I learned then that we were but few, while the white men were many, and that we could not hold our own with them. We were like deer. They were like grizzly bears. We had a small country. Their country was large. We were contented to let things remain as the Great Spirit Chief made them. They were not and would change the rivers and mountains if they did not suit them.

Year after year we were threatened, but no war was made upon my people until General Howard came to our country two years ago and told us that he was the white war-chief of all that country. He said, "I have a great many soldiers at my back. I am going to bring them up here, and then I will talk to you again. I will not let white men laugh at me the next time I come. This country belongs to the government, and I intend to make you go upon the reservation."

The next spring the agent at Umatilla Agency sent an Indian runner to tell me to meet General Howard at Walla Walla. I could not go myself, but I sent my brother and five other head men to meet him, and they had a long talk. General Howard said, "You have talked straight, and it is all right. You can stay at Wallowa." General Howard then sent out runners and called all the Indians to a grand council at Fort Lapwai. I was in that council. I said to General Howard, "We are ready to listen." He answered that he would not talk then, but would hold a council next day, when he would talk plainly. I said to General Howard, "I am ready to talk today. I have been in a great many councils, but I am no wiser. We are all sprung from one woman, although we are unlike in many things. We cannot be made over again. You are as you were made, and as you were made you can remain. We are just as we were made by the Great Spirit, and you cannot change us. Then why should children of one mother and one father quarrel? Why should one try to cheat the other? I do not believe that the Great Spirit Chief gave one kind of men the right to tell another kind of men what they must do."

16

Then one of my chiefs, Too-hool-hool-sote, rose and said to General Howard, "The Great Spirit Chief made the world as it is, and as He wanted it, and He made a part of it for us to live upon. I do not see where you get authority to say that we shall not live where He placed us."

General Howard lost his temper and said, "Shut up! I don't want to hear any more of such talk. The law says you shall go upon the reservation to live, and I want you to do so, but you persist in disobeying the law. If you do not move, I will take the matter into my own hand and make you suffer for your disobedience."

Too-hool-hool-sote answered, "Who are you that you ask us to talk and then tell me I shan't talk? Are you the Great Spirit? Did you make the world? Did you make the sun? Did you make the rivers to run for us to drink? Did you make the grass to grow? Did you make all these things that you talk to us as though we were boys? If you did, then you have the right to talk as you do."

General Howard replied, "You are an impudent fellow, and I will put you in the guardhouse," and then ordered a soldier to arrest him.

Too-hool-hool-sote made no resistance. He asked General Howard, "Is this your order? I don't care. I have expressed my heart to you. I have nothing to take back. I have spoken for my country. You can arrest me, but you cannot change me or make me take back what I have said."

The soldiers came forward, seized my friend, and took him to the guardhouse. My men whispered among themselves whether they would let this thing be done. I counseled them to submit. I knew if we resisted that all the white men present, including General Howard, would be killed in a moment, and we would be blamed. If I had said nothing, General Howard would not have been alive to give an unjust order against my men. I saw the danger and while they dragged Too-hool-hool-sote to prison, I arose and said, "I am going to talk now. I don't care whether you arrest me or not." I turned to my people and said, "The arrest of Too-hool-hool-sote was wrong, but we will not resent the insult. We were invited to this council to express our hearts, and we have done so." This ended the council that day. Too-hool-hool-sote was prisoner for five days before he was released.

18

On the next morning General Howard came to my lodge and invited me to go with him and White Bird and Looking Glass to look for land for my people. As we rode along we came to some good land that was already occupied by Indians and white people. General Howard, pointing to this land, said, "If you will come onto the reservation, I will give you these lands and move these people off."

I replied, "No. It would be wrong to disturb these people. I have no right to take their homes. I have never taken what did not belong to me. I will not now."

We rode all day upon the reservation and found no good land unoccupied. I have been informed by men who do not lie that General Howard sent a letter that night telling the soldiers at Walla Walla to go to Wallowa Valley and drive us out upon our return home.

In the council the next day General Howard informed us in a haughty spirit that he would give my people thirty days to go back home, collect all our stock, and move onto the reservation, saying, "If you are not here in that time, I shall consider that you want to fight and will send my soldiers to drive you on."

I said, "War can be avoided and ought to be avoided. I want no war. My people have always been the friends of the white man. Why are you in such a hurry? I cannot get ready to move in thirty days. Our stock is scattered, and Snake River is very high. Let us wait till fall when the river will be low. We want time to hunt our stock and gather our supplies for the winter."

General Howard replied, "If you let the time run over one day, the soldiers will be there to drive you onto the reservation, and all your cattle and horses outside of the reservation at that time will fall into the hands of the white men."

I knew I had never sold my country, but I did not want bloodshed. I did not want my people killed. I did not want anybody killed. I said in my heart that rather than have war, I would give up my country. I would rather give up my father's grave. I would give up everything rather than have the blood of white men upon the hands of my people.

When I returned to Wallowa, I found my people very much excited upon discovering that the soldiers were already in the Wallowa Valley. We held a council and decided to move immediately to avoid bloodshed.

Too-hool-hool-sote, who felt outraged by his imprisonment, talked for war and made many of my young men willing to fight rather than be driven like dogs from the land where they were born. He declared that blood alone would wash out the disgrace General Howard had put upon him. It required a strong heart to stand up against such talk, but I urged my people to be quiet and not to begin a war.

We gathered all the stock we could find and made an attempt to move. We left many of our horses and cattle in Wallowa and lost several hundred in crossing the river. All my people succeeded in getting across in safety. Many of the Nez Perces came together in Rocky Canyon to hold a grand council. I went with all my people. This council lasted ten days. There was a great deal of war talk and a great deal of excitement. There was one young brave present whose father had been killed by a white man five years before. This man's blood was bad against white men, and he left the council calling for revenge.

Again I counseled peace, and I thought the danger was past. We had not complied with General Howard's order because we could not, but we intended to do so as soon as possible. I was leaving the council to kill beef for my family when news came that the young man whose father had been killed had gone out with several hot-blooded young braves and killed four white men. He rode up to the council and shouted, "Why do you sit here like women? The war has already begun."

I was deeply grieved. All the lodges were moved except my brother's and my own. I saw clearly that the war was upon us when I learned that my young men had been secretly buying ammunition. I heard then that Too-hool-hool-sote, who had been imprisoned by General Howard, had succeeded in organizing a war party. I knew that their acts would involve all my people. I saw that the war could not then be prevented. The time had passed. I had counseled peace from the beginning. I knew that we were too weak to fight the United States. We had many grievances, but I knew that war would bring more.

There were bad men among my people who had quarreled with white men, and they talked of white men's wrongs until they roused all the bad hearts in the council. Still I could not believe that they would begin a war. I know that my young men did a great wrong, but I ask, who was first to blame? They had been insulted a thousand times. Their fathers and brothers had been killed; their mothers and wives had been disgraced; they had been driven to madness by the whiskey sold to them by the white men; they had been told by General Howard that all their horses and cattle which they had been unable to drive out of Wallowa were to fall into the hands of white men; and, added to all this, they were homeless and desperate.

I would have given my own life if I could have undone the killing of white men by my people. I blame my young men and I blame the white men. I blame General Howard for not giving my people time to get their stock away from Wallowa. I do not acknowledge that he had the right to order me to leave Wallowa at any time. I deny that either my father or I ever sold that land. It is still our land. It may never again be our home, but my father sleeps there, and I love it as I love my mother. I left there hoping to avoid bloodshed.

If General Howard had given me plenty of time to gather up my stock and had treated Too-hool-hool-sote as a man should be treated, there would have been no war. My friends among white men have blamed me for the war. I am not to blame. When my young men began the killing, my heart was hurt. Although I did not justify them, I remembered all the insults I had endured, and my blood was on fire. Still I would have taken my people to the buffalo country without fighting, if possible.

I could see no way to avoid a war. We moved over to White Bird Creek, sixteen miles away and there encamped, intending to collect our stock before leaving, but the soldiers attacked us and the first battle was fought. In that battle we numbered sixty men, and the soldiers a hundred. The fight lasted but a few minutes when the soldiers retreated before us for twelve miles. They lost thirty-three killed and had seven wounded. When an Indian fights, he only shoots to kill, but soldiers shoot at random. None of the soldiers was scalped. We do not believe in scalping nor in killing wounded men. Soldiers do not kill many Indians except when wounded have been left upon the battlefield. Then soldiers kill Indians.

Seven days after the initial battle General Howard arrived in the Nez Perces' country, bringing seven hundred more soldiers. It was now war in earnest. We crossed over Salmon River, hoping General Howard would follow. We were not disappointed. He did follow us, and we got between him and his supplies and cut him off for three days. He sent out two companies to open the way. We attacked them, killing one officer, two guides, and ten other men.

We withdrew, hoping the soldiers would follow, but they had had fighting enough for that day. They entrenched themselves, and next day we attacked again. The battle [near Cottonwood] lasted all day and was renewed the next morning. We killed four and wounded seven or eight.

After this time General Howard found out that we were in his rear. Five days later he attacked us with three hundred and fifty soldiers and settlers. We had two hundred and fifty warriors. The fight [at Cottonwood Creek] lasted twenty-seven hours. We lost four killed and several wounded. General Howard lost twenty-nine killed and sixty wounded.

The following day the soldiers charged upon us and we retreated with our families and stock a few miles [to Kamiah], leaving eighty lodges to fall into General Howard's hands.

Finding that we were outnumbered, we retreated into the Bitterroot Valley [in Montana]. Here another body of soldiers came upon us and demanded our surrender. We refused. They said, "You cannot get by us." We answered, "We are going by you without fighting if you will let us, but we are going by you anyhow." We then made a treaty with these soldiers. We agreed not to molest anyone and they agreed that we might pass through Bitterroot country in peace. We bought provisions and traded stock with white men there.

We understood that there was to be no further war. We intended to go peaceably to the buffalo country and leave the question of returning to our country to be settled afterward. With this understanding, we traveled on for four days, and thinking that the trouble was all over, we stopped and prepared tent poles to take with us. We started again, and at the end of two days we saw three white men passing our camp. Thinking that peace had been made, we did not molest them. We could have killed them or taken them prisoners, but we did not suspect them of being spies, which they were.

That night the soldiers surrounded our camp. About daybreak one of my men went out to look after his horses. The soldiers saw him and shot him down like a coyote. I have since learned that these soldiers were not those we had left behind. They had come upon us from another direction. The new white war-chief's name was Gibbon. He charged upon us while some of my people were still asleep. We had a hard fight. Some of my men crept around and attacked the soldiers from the rear. In this battle [at the Big Hole] we lost nearly all our lodges, but we finally drove General Gibbon back. In the fight we lost fifty women and children and thirty fighting men. We remained long enough to bury our dead.

The Nez Perces never make war on women and children. We could have killed a great many women and children while the war lasted, but we would feel ashamed to do so cowardly an act. We never scalp our enemies, but when General Howard came up and joined General Gibbon, their Indian scouts dug up our dead and scalped them.

We retreated as rapidly as we could toward the buffalo country. After six days General Howard came close to us, and we went out and attacked him and captured nearly all his horses and mules. We then marched on to the Yellowstone Basin.

Nine days' march brought us to the mouth of Clark's Fork of the Yellowstone River. We did not know what had become of General Howard, but we supposed that he had sent for more horses and mules. He did not come up, but another new war-chief [General Sturgis] attacked us. We held him in check while we moved all our women and children and stock out of danger, leaving a few men to cover our retreat.

Several days passed and we heard nothing of General Howard or Gibbon or Sturgis. We had repulsed each in turn and began to feel secure when another army, under General Miles, struck us. This was the fourth army that we had encountered, each of which outnumbered our fighting force.

We had no knowledge of General Miles' army until a short time before he charged upon us, cutting our camp in two and capturing nearly all of our horses. About seventy men, myself among them, were cut off. My little daughter, twelve years of age, was with me. I gave her a rope and told her to catch a horse and join those who were separated from the camp. I have not seen her since, but I have learned that she is alive and well.

I thought of my wife and my other children, now surrounded by soldiers, and I resolved to go to them or die. With a prayer to the Great Spirit Chief, I dashed unarmed through the line of soldiers. It seemed to me that there were guns on every side. My clothes were cut to pieces and my horse was wounded, but I was not hurt. As I reached the door of my lodge, my wife handed me my rifle, saying, "Here's your gun. Fight!"

The soldiers kept up a continuous fire. Six of my men were killed in one spot near me. Ten or twelve soldiers charged into our camp and got possession of two lodges, killing three Nez Perces and losing three of their men, who fell inside our lines. I called my men to drive them back. We fought at close range, not more than twenty steps apart, and drove the soldiers back upon their main line, leaving their dead in our hands. We secured their arms and ammunition. The first day and night we lost eighteen men and three women. General Miles lost twenty-six killed and forty wounded. On the following day General Miles sent a messenger into my camp under protection of a white flag. I sent my friend Yellow Bull to meet him.

Yellow Bull understood the messenger to say that General Miles wished me to consider the situation, that he did not want to kill my people unnecessarily. Yellow Bull understood this to be a demand for me to surrender and save blood. Upon reporting this message to me, Yellow Bull said he wondered whether General Miles was in earnest. I sent him back with my answer, that I had not made up my mind but would think about it and send word soon. A little later he sent some Cheyenne scouts with another message. I went out to meet them. They said they believed that General Miles was sincere and really wanted peace. I walked on to General Miles' tent. He met me and we shook hands. He said, "Come, let us sit down by the fire and talk this matter over." I remained with him all night. Next morning, Yellow Bull came over to see if I was alive and why I did not return. General Miles would not let me leave the tent to see my friend alone.

I did not make any agreement the next day with General Miles. The battle was renewed while I was with him. I was very anxious about my people. I knew that we were near Sitting Bull's camp in King George's land, and I thought maybe the Nez Perces who had escaped would return with assistance. No great damage was done to either party during the night.

On the following morning I returned to my camp by agreement, meeting the officer who had been held a prisoner in my camp at the flag of truce. My people were divided about surrendering. We could have escaped from Bear Paw Mountain if we had left our wounded, old women, and children behind. We were unwilling to do this. We had never heard of a wounded Indian recovering while in the hands of white men.

On the evening of the fourth day, General Howard came in with a small escort, together with my friend Chapman [an interpreter]. We could now talk understandingly. General Miles said to me in plain words, "If you will come out and give up your arms, I will spare your lives and send you back to the reservation." I do not know what passed between General Miles and General Howard.

I could not bear to see my wounded men and women suffer any longer; we had lost enough already. General Miles had promised that we might return to our country with what stock we had left. I thought we could start again. I believed General Miles, or I never would have surrendered. I have heard that he has been censured for making the promise to return us to Lapwai. He could not have made any other terms with me at that time. I would have held him in check until my friends came to my assistance, and then neither of the generals nor their soldiers would have ever left Bear Paw Mountain alive.

On the fifth day I went to General Miles and gave up my gun. My people needed rest. We wanted peace.

I was told we could go with General Miles to Tongue River and stay there until spring, when we would be sent back to our country. Finally it was decided that we were to be taken to Tongue River. We had nothing to say about it. After our arrival at Tongue River, General Miles received orders to take us to Bismarck [North Dakota]. The reason given was that subsistence would be cheaper there.

General Miles was opposed to this order. He said, "You must not blame me. I have endeavored to keep my word, but the chief who is over me has given the order, and I must obey it or resign. That would do you no good. Some other officer would carry out the order."

I believe General Miles would have kept his word if he could have done so. I do not blame him for what we have suffered since the surrender. I do not know who is to blame. We gave up all our horses—over eleven hundred, and all our saddles—over one hundred, and we have not heard of them since. Somebody has our horses.

General Miles turned my people over to another soldier and we were taken to Bismarck. Captain Johnson, who now had charge of us, received an order to take us to Fort Leavenworth [Kansas]. At Leavenworth we were placed on a low river bottom with no water except river water to drink and cook with. We had always lived in a healthy country where the mountains were high and the water was cold and clear. Many of our people sickened and died, and we buried them in this strange land. I cannot tell how much my heart suffered for my people while at Leavenworth. The Great Spirit Chief who rules above seemed to be looking some other way and did not see what was being done to my people.

During the hot days [July 1878], we received notice that we were to be moved farther away from our own country. We were not asked if we were willing to go. We were ordered to get into railroad cars. Three of my people died on the way to Baxter Springs [Kansas]. It was worse to die there than to die fighting in the mountains.

We were moved from Baxter Springs to the Indian Territory and set down without our lodges. We had but little medicine and were nearly all sick. Seventy of my people have died since we moved there.

The Commissioner Chief came to see us. I told him, as I told everyone, that I expected General Miles' word would be carried out. He said it could not be done, that white men now lived in my country, and all the land was taken up; that if I returned to Wallowa, I could not live in peace; that law papers were out against my young men who began the war; and that the government could not protect my people. This talk fell like a heavy stone upon my heart. I saw that I could not gain anything by talking to him. Other law chiefs (congressional committee) then came to see us and said they would help me get to a healthy country. I did not know whom to believe. The white people have too many chiefs. They do not understand each other. They do not talk alike.

At last I was granted permission to come to Washington. I am glad I came. I have shaken hands with a great many friends, but there are some things I wanted to know which no one seems able to explain. I cannot understand how the government sends a man out to fight us, as it did General Miles, and then breaks his word. Such a government has something wrong about it. I cannot understand why so many chiefs are allowed to talk so many different ways and promise so many different things. I have heard talk and talk, but nothing is done. Good words do not last long until they amount to something. Words do not pay for my dead people. They do not pay for my land, now overrun by white men. They do not protect my father's grave. They do not pay for my horses and cattle. Good words will not give me back my children. Good words will not make good the promise of your War Chief, General Miles. Good words will not give my people health. Good words will not get my people a home where they can live in peace and take care of themselves. I am tired of talk that comes to nothing. It makes my heart sick when I remember all the good words and all the broken promises.

41

If the white man wants to live in peace with the Indian, he can live in peace. There need be no trouble. Treat all men alike. Give them all the same law. Give them all an even chance to live and grow. All men were made by the same Great Spirit Chief. They are all brothers. The earth is the mother of all people, and all people should have equal rights upon it. You may as well expect the rivers to run backward as that any man who was born a free man should be contented while penned up and denied liberty to go where he pleases. If you tie a horse to a stake, do you expect he will grow fat? If you pen an Indian up on a small spot of earth and compel him to stay there, he will not be contented nor will he grow and prosper. I have asked some of the great white chiefs where they get their authority to say to the Indian that he shall stay in one place, while he sees white men going where they please. They cannot tell me.

I only ask of the Government to be treated as all other men are treated. If I cannot go to my own home, let me have a home in some country where my people will not die so fast. I would like to go to Bitterroot Valley. There my people would be healthy. Where they are now, they are dying. Three have died since I left my camp to come to Washington.

When I think of our condition, my heart is heavy. I see men of my race treated as outlaws, driven from country to country, or shot down like animals.

I know that my race must change. We cannot hold our own with the white men as we are. We only ask an even chance to live as other men live. We ask to be recognized as men. We ask that the same law shall work alike on all men. If the Indian breaks the law, punish him by the law. If the white man breaks the law, punish him also.

Let me be a free man—free to travel, free to stop, free to work, free to trade where I choose, free to choose my own teachers, free to follow the religion of my fathers, free to think and talk and act for myself—and I will obey every law or submit to the penalty.

Whenever the white man treats the Indian as they treat each other, then we shall have no more wars. We shall be all alike—brothers of one father and one mother, with one sky above us and one country around us and one government for all. Then the Great Spirit Chief who rules above will smile upon this land and send rain to wash out the bloody spots made by brothers' hands upon the face of the earth. No more groans of wounded men and women will ever go to the ear of the Great Spirit Chief above, and all people may be one people.

In-mut-too-yah-lat-lat
has spoken for his people.

Timeline

1805 Nez Perces' first documented contact with whites (Lewis and Clark Party); Nez Perce oral history spoke of earlier contact with white trappers and traders.

1836 Reverend Henry Spalding's mission site established in Nez Perce country.

1840 Birth of Young Chief Joseph.

1855 Nez Perce and other Northwest Indian reservations established by treaties.

1863 Nez Perce Indian Reservation reduced by treaty, from 1855 delineation of 10,000 square miles to a little more than 1,000, in a process through which the Nez Perces became split into "treaty" and "nontreaty" factions.

1871 Old Chief Joseph died; Young Chief Joseph became chief of his band.

1877

Early in year Gen. O.O. Howard began an endeavor to force the nontreaty Nez Perces to move within reservation boundaries.

Early June, complying nontreaty bands assembled just outside reservation boundaries.

June 13th, group of young warriors slew five Salmon River settlers.

Looking Glass removed his band onto reservation land near the mouth of Clear Creek; White Bird, Too-hool-hool-sote, and Joseph took their bands to Whitebird Creek Canyon about a mile from the Salmon River.

June 17th, Capt. David Perry, with two companies of cavalry and eleven settler volunteers, attacked the Whitebird Canyon encampment; the U.S. Army lost thirty-four soldiers and two volunteers, the Nez Perces lost no warriors.

June 22nd, Gen. Howard with slightly more than two hundred soldiers, twenty volunteers and packers and guides set out in pursuit of the nontreaties; the Nez Perces had by now crossed to the west side of the Salmon.

July 1st, Gen. Howard and company reached the Salmon and next day crossed to the west side; by this time the nontreaties had returned to the east side of the river farther downstream.

Same day, Capt. Whipple, under orders, attempted arrest of Looking Glass and his warriors along Clear Creek, but a battle ensued, after which Looking Glass, enraged at being attacked, refused to remain cooperative.

July 3rd, Lieutenant Sevier M. Rains and a detail of ten soldiers and one civilian, attempting rescue of another civilian, were slain east of Cottonwood by an advance guard of the nontreaty Nez Perces.

July 4th, group of Nez Perces surrounded soldiers and settlers at Cottonwood where a day-long battle was then enjoined.

July 5th, two attacks against civilian whites in the Cottonwood area.

July 8th, having also recrossed the Salmon, Gen. Howard's company reached Grangeville; the nontreaties were by then camped at the mouth of Cottonwood Creek on the South Fork of the Clearwater River, along with the Red Owl and Looking Glass bands, who had joined them a few days earlier.

July 11th, Gen. Howard, with approximately four hundred soldiers and one hundred volunteers, located the nontreaty encampment, and the "Battle of the Clearwater" ensued.

Late next day, having lost four warriors and suffered six wounded, the Nez Perces retreated up Cottonwood Creek; the Army had lost fifteen and suffered twenty-five wounded.

By the following day when the Army pursued them, the nontreaties had reached the Kamiah Valley and crossed the main Clearwater River and by July 15th, reached the Weippe Prairie.

July 16th, the nontreaty Nez Perces began trek eastward along the Lolo Trail.

July 27th, having constructed a crude log barricade, Capt. Charles Rawn, with soldiers, civilian volunteers, and Flathead Indians, attempted to peaceably stop the Nez Perce line, which was emerging from the Lolo Trail.

July 28th, Rawn and company awoke to see the Nez Perces passing along a high ridge into Montana's Bitterroot country, successfully circumventing the barricade.

July 30th, Gen. Howard with seven hundred men set out along the Lolo Trail to follow the nontreaties eastward.

August 7th, the Nez Perces reached Big Hole Valley in Montana and camped; Gen. Howard and company were still on the Lolo Trail.

August 8th, 163 Montana infantry troops and thirty-four volunteers surprise attacked the Nez Perces' camp at dawn, killing nearly ninety Nez Perces, including many women and children.

Same day, the head of Gen. Howard's line reached Lolo Creek in Montana and on the 9th proceded into the Bitterroot Valley.

August 10th, having rallied, killing thirty-one whites and wounding forty, the Nez Perces held off the soldiers at the Big Hole from further attack and began moving southward and later east into Yellowstone National Park.

August 20th, group of warriors stampeded Gen. Howard's mule herd, causing Howard to halt to retreive mules, while the Nez Perces wound their way northeastward, out-witting along the way several companies of troops organized to block their passage via various routes.

Second week in September, Nez Perces reached the Yellowstone River, fifty miles ahead of Gen. Howard.

September 13th, Col. Samuel Sturgis, with six companies, overtook the Nez Perces at Canyon Creek near present-day Billings; rear guard of Nez Perce warriors held them off in a series of skirmishes as the main group of Indians continued northward.

September 29th, Nez Perces stopped near the Bear Paw Mountains, forty miles south of the Canadian border.

September 30th predawn, Col. Nelson Miles' command attacked the Nez Perces' camp; fifty-three soldiers were lost.

For five days the Nez Perces skirmished with Miles' troops; one-fourth to one-third of the remaining Nez Perces escaped to Canada.

Intermittently, throughout the stand-off, Miles attempted to negotiate a surrender among the Nez Perce chiefs, promising them they could return to the Clearwater country if they surrendered.

October 4th, Looking Glass was killed; Gen. Howard arrived later in the day with an advance group of his command; and in the late afternoon, Joseph and five others rode into the military camp to surrender.

Following the war, the Nez Perces were taken as prisoners of war to Fort Leavenworth, Kansas, where twenty-one died of malaria.

1878 the Nez Perce prisoners were moved to Baxter Springs, Kansas, then later to northeastern Oklahoma; Chief Joseph continually appealed to government officials to let his people return to their homeland.

1879, January, Chief Joseph was granted a visit with President Rutherford Hays and the right to address an assembly of officials in Washington, D.C.; Idaho settlers successfully lobbied for continuation of the non-treaties' exile.

1883 Nez Perce Presbyterian James Reuben was allowed to take two elderly men and twenty seven women and children back to Clearwater country.

1884 U.S. Congress authorized the return of the remaining Nez Perce exiles to the Northwest.

1885, in May, one hundred fifty Nez Perce exiles, including Joseph, were taken to the Colville Reservation in northeastern Washington; one hundred eighteen to the Nez Perce Reservation in north central Idaho.

September 21, 1904, Chief Joseph died on the Colville Reservation of, according to the attending physician, a broken heart.